EXPLORING
WEATHER

METEOROLOGISTS AT WORK!

ELSIE OLSON

Consulting Editor, Diane Craig, M.A./Reading Specialist

Super Sandcastle

An Imprint of Abdo Publishing
abdopublishing.com

abdopublishing.com

Printed in the United States of America, North Mankato, Minnesota

102017
012018

THIS BOOK CONTAINS RECYCLED MATERIALS

Design: Kelly Doudna, Mighty Media, Inc.
Production: Mighty Media, Inc.
Editor: Jessie Alkire
Cover Photographs: NASA; NASA's Goddard Space Flight Center; Wikimedia Commons
Interior Photographs: iStockphoto; NASA's Goddard Space Flight Center; Shutterstock; Wellcome Library, London; Wikimedia Commons

Publisher's Cataloging-in-Publication Data

Names: Olson, Elsie, author.
Title: Exploring weather: meteorologists at work! / by Elsie Olson.
Other titles: Meteorologists at work!
Description: Minneapolis, Minnesota : Abdo Publishing, 2018. | Series: Earth detectives |
Identifiers: LCCN 2017946514 | ISBN 9781532112348 (lib.bdg.) | ISBN 9781614799764 (ebook)
Subjects: LCSH: Meteorology--Juvenile literature. | Weather forecasting--Juvenile literature. |
    Occupations--Juvenile literature. | Earth sciences--Juvenile literature.
Classification: DDC 551.5--dc23
LC record available at https://lccn.loc.gov/2017946514

Super SandCastle™ books are created by a team of professional educators, reading specialists, and content developers around five essential components—phonemic awareness, phonics, vocabulary, text comprehension, and fluency—to assist young readers as they develop reading skills and strategies and increase their general knowledge. All books are written, reviewed, and leveled for guided reading, early reading intervention, and Accelerated Reader™ programs for use in shared, guided, and independent reading and writing activities to support a balanced approach to literacy instruction.

CONTENTS

What Is Weather? 4

Who Studies Weather? 6

John Dalton 8

Weather Tracking 10

Forecasts 12

Extreme Weather 14

Climate Science 16

A Meteorologist's Tool Kit 18

Future Forecasts 20

Become a Meteorologist! 22

Test Your Knowledge 23

Glossary 24

WHAT IS WEATHER?

Weather is the state of the atmosphere in one time and place. This means how hot or cold it is. It also means if it is rainy, sunny, or cloudy.

The sun's heat causes weather. So do air movement and moisture. Landforms also affect weather. Mountains block wind. This can slow down storms.

WHO STUDIES WEATHER?

Some scientists study weather. They are called meteorologists. They work in weather stations. These are all over the world!

Some meteorologists **predict** weather. They warn people about storms. Others study climate. Climate is the average weather in an area.

Some meteorologists work for TV stations.

Some US meteorologists work for the National Weather Service. The National Weather Service provides information to help people prepare for storms.

JOHN DALTON

John Dalton was a famous meteorologist. He was born in England in 1766. His family was very poor.

John loved learning. He went to a local school. But he started teaching others when he was 12! John taught himself science and math. He studied topics such as color blindness and atoms.

When John was 14, he became a farmhand in his village in Cumberland, England. But after a year, he decided to return to science and teaching.

WEATHER TRACKING

Dalton is called the father of **meteorology**. He started keeping weather records in 1787. He wrote weather reports every day. He did this for his whole life!

Dalton made weather tools. He measured wind speed and air pressure. He also tracked temperature and **humidity**. Scientists still use Dalton's data.

JOHN DALTON

BORN: September 6, 1766, Eaglesfield, England

MARRIED: Never married

CHILDREN: None

DIED: July 27, 1844, Manchester, England

FORECASTS

Meteorologists use computer models to study weather. Models collect data from many sources. One source is **radar**. This shows weather patterns over a large area.

Models help make weather forecasts. Forecasts cover days or weeks. Some go out for months! They help people plan.

Doppler radar towers collect information about weather.

Meteorologists use radar to create special maps. These maps show the paths of storms and precipitation such as rain, hail, and snow.

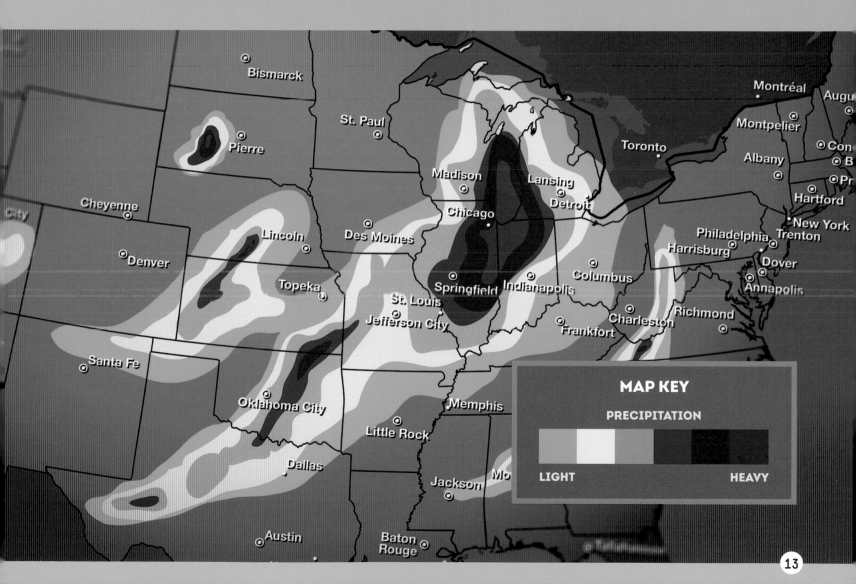

MAP KEY

PRECIPITATION

LIGHT   HEAVY

EXTREME WEATHER

Sometimes meteorologists forecast **extreme** weather. This can be heat waves or floods. It can also be storms. **Tornadoes** and **hurricanes** are storms. These events cause **damage**. They can hurt or kill people.

Meteorologists try to **predict** where and when extreme weather will happen. Then they can warn people.

Tornado

CLIMATE SCIENCE

Not all weather scientists make forecasts. Some study climate. They look at long-term weather patterns. These scientists study how and why patterns change.

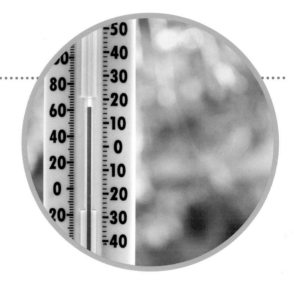

Scientists watch global temperatures closely.

Earth's climate is slowly getting warmer. This could lead to more **extreme** weather. It could cause sea levels to rise. This would flood coastal cities. Scientists look at ways people can slow this change.

Temperatures in the Arctic are rising more quickly than the rest of the world. Arctic sea ice is also decreasing quickly.

A METEOROLOGIST'S TOOL KIT

BAROMETER
This measures air pressure. Changes in pressure can mean changes in weather.

RAIN GAUGE
This collects rain. It shows how much rain falls over time.

Meteorologists use tools to measure and track weather.

THERMOMETER
This measures the air temperature.

WEATHER SATELLITE
Weather **satellites** orbit Earth. They take images of clouds and storms and send the images back to Earth.

FUTURE FORECASTS

Studying weather is not easy. Scientists may disagree on what climate patterns mean. Forecasts aren't always right. Models sometimes miss the path of storms.

But tools keep improving. **Drones** can get closer to storms than scientists can. Drones fly above storms and gather data. They send the data back to scientists. Forecasts will be more **accurate** than ever!

Today, people can view weather **radar** maps **online**. They can make their own weather **predictions**.

People who follow storms to take photos or videos are called storm chasers. These people can stay safe in storms by using drones!

BECOME A METEOROLOGIST!

Do you dream of becoming a meteorologist? Here are some things you can do now!

TAKE SCIENCE AND MATH CLASSES. Studying weather involves math and science. Getting good grades in those classes now will help you in the future.

PRACTICE YOUR WRITING AND SPEAKING SKILLS. Meteorologists need to clearly explain forecasts. They also give presentations about their research.

ASK QUESTIONS! Scientists ask a lot of questions. They look for new ways to find answers. You can get started now!

TEST YOUR KNOWLEDGE

1. What type of scientist studies weather?

2. In what year did John Dalton begin keeping weather records?

3. Climate scientists study weather patterns over a long period of time. **TRUE OR FALSE?**

THINK ABOUT IT!

What is the climate like where you live? What is the weather like today?

ANSWERS: 1. Meteorologist 2. 1787 3. True

GLOSSARY

accurate – exact or correct.

damage – harm or ruin.

drone – an aircraft or ship that is controlled by radio signals.

extreme – exceeding the ordinary or expected.

humidity – the amount of moisture in the air.

hurricane – a tropical storm with very high winds that starts in the ocean and moves toward land.

meteorology – the study of weather.

online – connected to the Internet.

predict – to guess something ahead of time on the basis of observation, experience, or reasoning. This guess is called a prediction.

radar – an instrument that uses the reflection of radio waves to detect and track objects.

satellite – a manufactured object that orbits Earth. It relays information back to Earth.

tornado – a destructive windstorm, usually with a funnel cloud.

8/19